Teacher's Notes
for Guided Reading

Oliver Twist

Teacher's notes by Alison Kelly
Roehampton University
and Suzanne Maile
Sheen Mount School

Contents

Essential information

National Curriculum level: 4A

Genre: classic text set in another era

Word count: 2,918

Interest words and phrases

workhouse	dormitory	gruel	apprentice
insolent	mute	urchins	gnarled
leering	drawled	helter–skelter	inscription
locket	brandished	grass	gristle
ladle	crossfire	cobbles	

Background

The appeal of *Oliver Twist*, first published in 1838, is enduring. Dickens paints a vivid picture of Victorian London which provides the backdrop for a memorable cast of characters, ranging from the truly evil Bill Sykes to the benevolent Mr. Brownlow. A rollercoaster plot, in which Oliver finds himself flung from abject misery to apparent salvation and back, is also a passionate indictment of Victorian poverty and those who exploit its victims. This retelling skilfully retains the essence of Dickens' plot, characterisation and language whilst providing a more accessible version for the age range.

Introducing the story

Before you start the reading session or sessions, spend a little time preparing with your group. Start by reading the information about Charles Dickens at the back of the book, drawing attention particularly to his childhood experience in a factory and the impact that had on his writing.

- If possible, collect pictures of Victorian London to share with the children. Try to include pictures of both poor and wealthy areas, showing the contrast between Fagin's slums and Mr. Brownlow's elegant townhouse.
- Discuss the appalling conditions in which many children lived at that time, and the expectation that they would work.
- Explain that there are many facts in the story that tell us about life in Victorian London.
- If necessary, remind the children of the distinction between 'fact' and 'fiction'.

Find out if the children know the story already, maybe through a film or stage version.

Tell the children that Dickens is famous for his creation of larger-than-life characters. Do they think that a retelling will try to do this as well? Discuss how an author can use figurative language (e.g. alliteration, similes, metaphors) to create settings and characters.

Look at the picture of Oliver on the front cover, and ask the children to help you create a word map to describe him. Your map might start looking like this:

thin

pale

boy   **OLIVER**

looks as if he's seen a ghost

Include examples of figurative language, and tell the children they will be looking out for more of these as the story unfolds.

Share learning objectives with your group.

The children are going to learn or practise the following:
- distinguishing between fact and fiction.
- understanding how settings and characters are built up from small details.

You might say:
- We are going to look at whether details in a story are also true in real life.
- We are going to see how an author uses lots of small details to build up a bigger picture of a character or a place, and make them seem real.

Now go on to the Walkthrough (see over the page).

Walkthrough

The walkthrough allows you to "warm" the text for the children by taking them through it without actually reading it.

- You might use it to identify key vocabulary, language patterns and concepts that children could need support with;
- It can be a way to identify key "thinking points" in the story (for example where predictions might be made, characters' thoughts inferred and so on).

Using a copy of the book, look through it with the children. We have suggested pause points and prompts.

Start by talking through Chapter 1 (pages 3-6).

You might ask:

- Where is the opening scene set?

- Read the description of the workhouse on page 4 ("a cold, grim place for the homeless without a spark of comfort or a crumb of nourishing food").

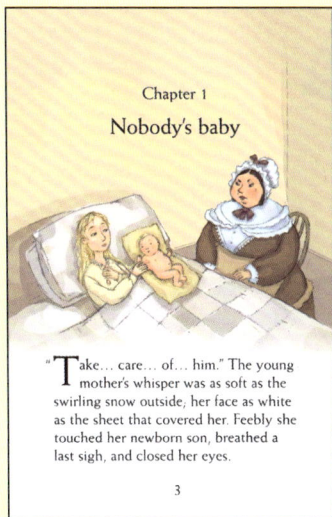

Chapter 1

Nobody's baby

"Take... care... of... him." The young mother's whisper was as soft as the swirling snow outside; her face as white as the sheet that covered her. Feebly she touched her newborn son, breathed a last sigh, and closed her eyes.

3

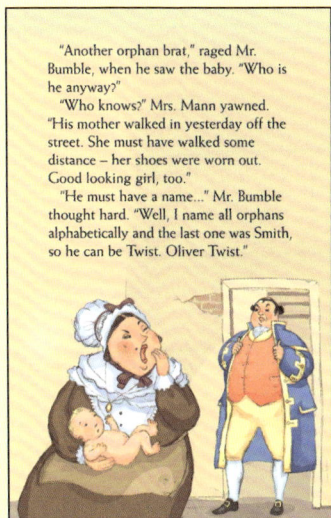

"Another orphan brat," raged Mr. Bumble, when he saw the baby. "Who is he anyway?"

"Who knows?" Mrs. Mann yawned. "His mother walked in yesterday off the street. She must have walked some distance – her shoes were worn out. Good looking girl, too."

"He must have a name..." Mr. Bumble thought hard. "Well, I name all orphans alphabetically and the last one was Smith, so he can be Twist. Oliver Twist."

page 5

- How has the illustrator drawn our attention to the different types of characters?
(Note the contrast between Mr. Bumble's colourful outfit and florid complexion with the muted grey shades of the workhouse.)

> "Ooh, Mr. Bumble, you are clever," smiled Mrs. Mann, fluttering her eyelashes at him. She wrapped Oliver in a scrap of cloth, yellowed with age.
>
> Oliver opened his mouth and roared with all the force of his baby lungs. If he'd understood he was an orphan, loved by no one, he would have cried even louder.

page 6

- Point out the characters who are introduced in the first chapter (Oliver's dying mother, Oliver, Mrs. Mann and Mr. Bumble) and ask the children what is fact in this chapter and what is fiction (i.e. the setting is factual but the characters are fictitious).

Now talk through Chapter 2 (pages 7-12).

- Note how the author helps us to read the dialogue through the use of strong verbs such as "complained" and "bellowed", and practise saying the lines with expression to fit these.

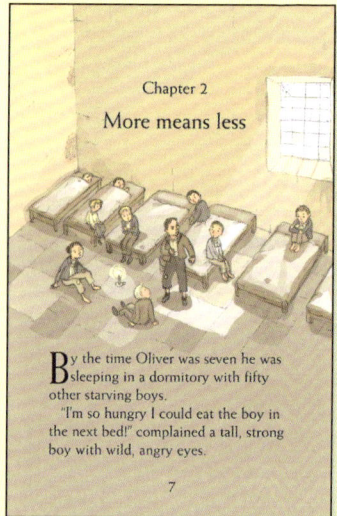

Chapter 2

More means less

> By the time Oliver was seven he was sleeping in a dormitory with fifty other starving boys.
>
> "I'm so hungry I could eat the boy in the next bed!" complained a tall, strong boy with wild, angry eyes.

7

The boy in the next bed gulped. "We must have more food," he agreed, hastily. "Let's draw straws to decide who's going to ask Mr. Bumble."

Oliver's heart was thumping as he reached out to draw his straw. He pulled it close. "Oh no!" he cried. "It's me."

Supper, as usual, was gruel – a kind of thin watery porridge with a few lumps of gristle floating in it. The boys lined up in front of Mr. Bumble who stood at one end of the dining room, a huge apron tied around his fat belly, ladling a small spoonful into each boy's bowl.

They returned to their tables to eat their food, packed on benches as tight as sardines, though not so plump. Their bowls never needed washing.

They were licked clean in seconds until they shone like polished china.

The boys sitting near Oliver kicked him under the table.

"Go on, Oliver."

"Ask NOW."

Shivering with fear, Oliver walked the length of the room. He clutched his bowl so tightly his knuckles gleamed white.

pages 8-9

A terrible silence descended, pierced by Oliver's slow echoing footsteps on the stone floor. He passed table after table of boys, their spoons laid down, their empty bowls in front of them. Each round-eyed boy stared at him expectantly as he went by. Oliver guessed what they were thinking – *I'm glad it's him, not me.*

At last he reached Mr. Bumble, who looked down his nose at Oliver, as though he were an insect he wanted to squash.

Oliver forced himself to speak. "Please sir, I want some more," he whispered.

"WHAT?" shouted Mr. Bumble.

"Please sir, I want some more."

Mr. Bumble swelled like an evil giant. His eyes bulged with fury and his face went purple. "More? How DARE you! Wicked boy!"

He seized Oliver, hit him with the gruel ladle and threw him into the coal cellar, locking the door. "Your punishment starts here," he bellowed.

Oliver heard him stump up the steps, muttering as he went. "No one's *ever* asked for more before. Mark my words, he'll be a criminal when he grows up. That boy will hang!"

11

9

Now go on to Chapter 3 (pages 13-21)

- Ask the children who might buy Oliver – and why.
- If necessary, explain about children being used as chimney sweeps and "mutes" at funerals. Many children also worked in factories or mines, cleaning dangerous machinery and crawling through narrow, dark tunnels.

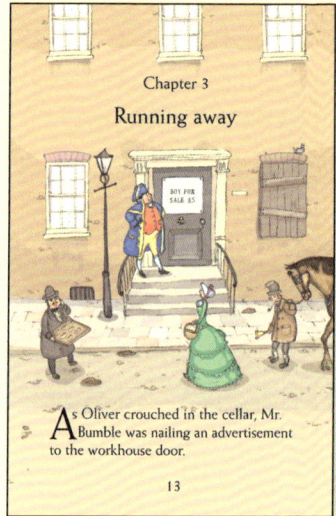

Chapter 3

Running away

As Oliver crouched in the cellar, Mr. Bumble was nailing an advertisement to the workhouse door.

13

The next day, Mr. Bumble dragged Oliver from the cellar. "There are two men coming to see you," he said, "so make sure you behave."

Oliver watched as the first man pulled up outside the door, in a donkey cart laden with soot.

"Whoah!" he shouted, hitting the donkey on the head with a great thump from his whip.

"Mr. Gamfield," said Mr. Bumble, stepping out to greet him.

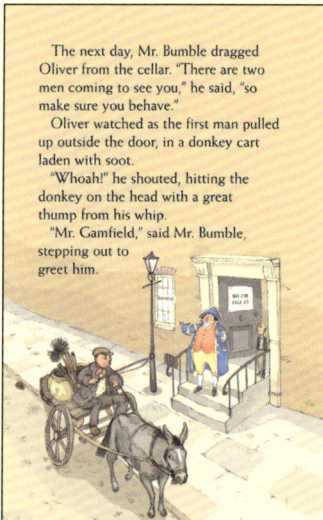

Mr. Gamfield stared at Oliver. "He's a very *small* boy. But I need an apprentice to climb chimneys and sweep out soot. Some of the chimneys are narrow and twisting. This brat will fit nicely."

"Please don't make me go," cried Oliver. "I won't go with him! I won't!"

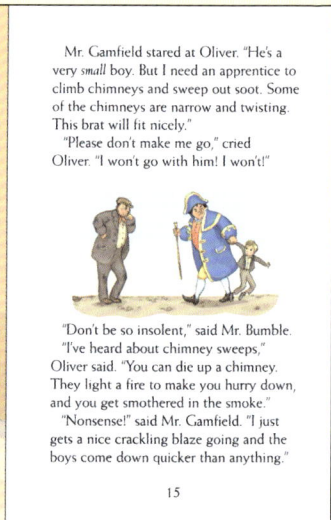

"Don't be so insolent," said Mr. Bumble.

"I've heard about chimney sweeps," Oliver said. "You can die up a chimney. They light a fire to make you hurry down, and you get smothered in the smoke."

"Nonsense!" said Mr. Gamfield. "I just gets a nice crackling blaze going and the boys come down quicker than anything."

15

"Then I'll frizzle in flames. I'm not going," replied Oliver firmly.

Mr. Gamfield clambered back into his donkey cart. "I don't want a rebellious boy. You've spoiled him, Mr. Bumble."

With that, he whipped the donkey until it trotted away.

Mr. Bumble shook Oliver until his teeth rattled. "Keep your mouth shut or no one will want you," he bellowed. "You've ruined that chance. Don't ruin the next. Look! Here it comes now."

He pointed to a thin, spidery man coming up to the door.

The man had a gloomy air. "I am Mr. Sowerberry," he introduced himself. "I arrange funerals and I need help." He looked at Oliver closely. "This boy will do, but he's so thin, he's not worth five pounds. I'll give you three pounds for him. Take it or leave it."

16

Mr. Bumble was disgusted, but there was nothing he could do. He was eager to see the last of Oliver. "Glad you're going, Oliver. Behave, or else..." he threatened.

Back at his shop, Mr. Sowerberry showed Oliver a dusty basement. A dim light filtered in, through a grimy pane of glass barred with rusty iron rails.

"You'll sleep here, you little bag of bones," he said.

Oliver looked around the shadowy room. It was stacked with empty coffins and planks of wood. Drapes of black cloth hung from hooks in the walls, billowing occasionally in the breeze, as though first they breathed... and then were lifeless. The only place to sleep – a recess behind the coffins where a thin mattress was thrust – looked like a grave.

"And this is Noah, my apprentice," Mr. Sowerberry went on, taking him to the kitchen. "Noah, give Oliver his supper."

Noah looked cross. "What work is he going to do?" he asked, sulkily.

"He'll be a mute. He's a good-looking boy. Dressed in a top hat and mourning clothes, he'll be a credit to the business."

"Please sir, what's a mute?" asked Oliver.

"A mute walks next to the coffin at funerals and follows it to the grave. Children's funerals only. Winter's coming on – the sickly season. Always lots of children's funerals this time of year..."

Noah grinned unpleasantly when Mr. Sowerberry left them alone. "Here's your food." He handed Oliver the dog's bowl. Stuck to the side were some stinking scraps of cold fat the dog had rejected.

Oliver was so hungry, he wolfed them down.

pages 18-19

"Pig!" mocked Noah. "Workhouse Boy! If your mother hadn't died, she'd be in prison. She must have been bad. Only bad 'uns give birth in the workhouse."

"Don't you dare say anything against my mother!" shouted Oliver.

"So? What are you going to do about it?" Noah jeered.

"This!" Oliver punched Noah hard in his flabby stomach. Noah collapsed like a crumpled balloon.

20

"Ow!" he squealed. "HELP! MURDER! Mr. Sowerberry? You've lost your mind, Oliver Twist. You just wait, Workhouse Boy. You'll be punished for this."

"Do what you want," replied Oliver. "I'm not staying here any longer." He raced out of the door and tore down the road, his heart pounding. "Don't let them come after me," he prayed.

The children should now be ready to read independently. This can be done over several sessions, depending on their experience and ability. We have allowed for three sessions, but you might take more or fewer.

Independent reading and strategy check

Before the children begin reading, include a strategy check to help them tackle difficult or unfamiliar words. **You might say:**

- Let's remember what we do when we can't read a word.
  Elicit suggestions from the children, e.g. blend the phonemes, read ahead.

Ask the children to read aloud, a little at a time, either all together or in turns, whilst you listen and monitor. Encourage them to use cues to work out unfamiliar words, and praise fluent reading or good use of strategies.

For assessment purposes, you may want to use the chart on pages 40-41 to note strategies that each child uses, or errors or comments that he or she makes, during the reading.

Now ask the children to read chapters 1-3 (pages 3-21) whilst you monitor and record strategies.

Chapter 1

Nobody's baby

"Take... care... of... him." The young mother's whisper was as soft as the swirling snow outside; her face as white as the sheet that covered her. Feebly she touched her newborn son, breathed a last sigh, and closed her eyes.

3

"She's dead!" announced Mrs. Mann, the midwife. "What a nuisance. I'll have to get Mr. Bumble."

Mr. Bumble was in charge of the workhouse – a cold, grim place for the homeless without a spark of comfort or a crumb of nourishing food. He didn't care if the inmates starved, as long as his own tummy felt warm and full three times a day.

Quickly, Mrs. Mann unclasped a gold locket from the dead woman's neck and put it around her own. Opening it, she read the name "Agnes" engraved inside.

"Another orphan brat," raged Mr. Bumble, when he saw the baby. "Who is he anyway?"

"Who knows?" Mrs. Mann yawned. "His mother walked in yesterday off the street. She must have walked some distance – her shoes were worn out. Good looking girl, too."

"He must have a name..." Mr. Bumble thought hard. "Well, I name all orphans alphabetically and the last one was Smith, so he can be Twist. Oliver Twist."

pages 4-5

"Ooh, Mr. Bumble, you are clever,"
smiled Mrs. Mann, fluttering her
eyelashes at him. She wrapped Oliver in
a scrap of cloth, yellowed with age.

Oliver opened his mouth and roared
with all the force of his baby lungs. If
he'd understood he was an orphan,
loved by no one, he would have cried
even louder.

Chapter 2

More means less

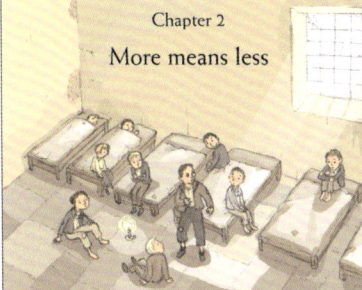

By the time Oliver was seven he was
sleeping in a dormitory with fifty
other starving boys.

"I'm so hungry I could eat the boy in
the next bed!" complained a tall, strong
boy with wild, angry eyes.

7

The boy in the next bed gulped. "We
must have more food," he agreed, hastily.
"Let's draw straws to decide who's going
to ask Mr. Bumble."

Oliver's heart was thumping as he
reached out to draw his straw. He pulled
it close. "Oh no!" he cried. "It's me."

Supper, as usual, was gruel – a kind of
thin watery porridge with a few lumps of
gristle floating in it. The boys lined up in
front of Mr. Bumble who stood at one
end of the dining room, a huge apron
tied around his fat belly, ladling a small
spoonful into each boy's bowl.

They returned to their tables to
eat their food, packed on benches
as tight as sardines, though not
so plump. Their bowls
never needed
washing.

They were licked clean in seconds until
they shone like polished china.

The boys sitting near Oliver kicked
him under the table.

"Go on, Oliver."

"Ask NOW."

Shivering with fear, Oliver walked
the length of the room. He clutched
his bowl so tightly his knuckles
gleamed white.

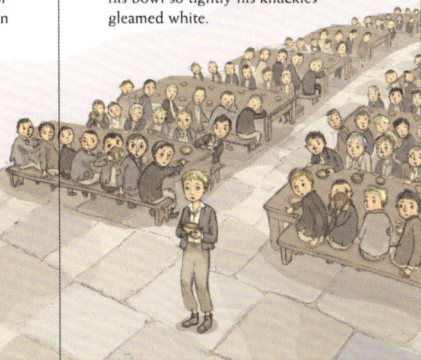

pages 8-9

15

A terrible silence descended, pierced by Oliver's slow echoing footsteps on the stone floor. He passed table after table of boys, their spoons laid down, their empty bowls in front of them. Each round-eyed boy stared at him expectantly as he went by. Oliver guessed what they were thinking – *I'm glad it's him, not me.*

At last he reached Mr. Bumble, who looked down his nose at Oliver, as though he were an insect he wanted to squash.

Oliver forced himself to speak. "Please sir, I want some more," he whispered.

"WHAT?" shouted Mr. Bumble.

"Please sir, I want some more."

Mr. Bumble swelled like an evil giant. His eyes bulged with fury and his face went purple. "More? How DARE you! Wicked boy!"

He seized Oliver, hit him with the gruel ladle and threw him into the coal cellar, locking the door. "Your punishment starts here," he bellowed.

Oliver heard him stump up the steps, muttering as he went. "No one's *ever* asked for more before. Mark my words, he'll be a criminal when he grows up. That boy will hang!"

In the dark, sooty cellar, cobwebs stroked Oliver's face like creepy fingers, and rats scratched the walls. He crouched in a corner, pressing himself close to the wall. Its hard, cold surface felt almost protective in the lonely gloom. He stayed awake all night, dreading what would happen to him next.

Pause after page 12.

Ask the children to find the similes that add to the descriptions in these pages (for example, "Mr. Bumble swelled like an evil giant" and "cobwebs stroked Oliver's face like creepy fingers").

You might ask:

- How do these similes help the reader?
- What do you think the boys might say in the dormitory that night whilst Oliver is in the cellar?
- Check the children understand "Its hard, cold surface felt almost protective in the lonely gloom".
- What might Oliver's thoughts be during that long, cold night?

Now ask the children to read on to page 15.

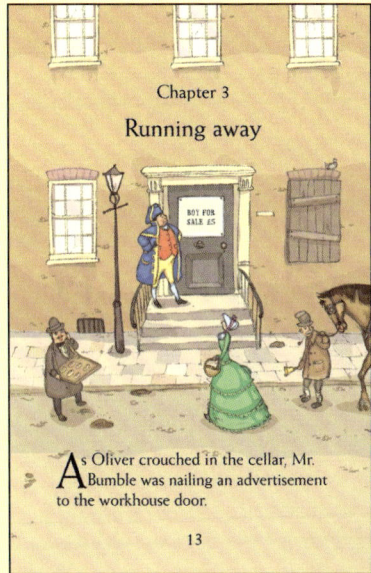

Chapter 3

Running away

BOY FOR
SALE £5

As Oliver crouched in the cellar, Mr.
Bumble was nailing an advertisement
to the workhouse door.

13

The next day, Mr. Bumble dragged Oliver from the cellar. "There are two men coming to see you," he said, "so make sure you behave."

Oliver watched as the first man pulled up outside the door, in a donkey cart laden with soot.

"Whoah!" he shouted, hitting the donkey on the head with a great thump from his whip.

"Mr. Gamfield," said Mr. Bumble, stepping out to greet him.

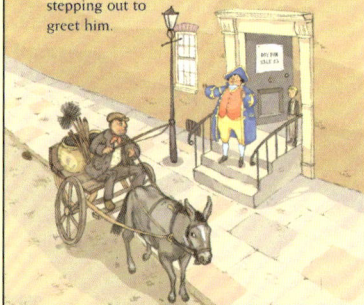

Mr. Gamfield stared at Oliver. "He's a very *small* boy. But I need an apprentice to climb chimneys and sweep out soot. Some of the chimneys are narrow and twisting. This brat will fit nicely."

"Please don't make me go," cried Oliver. "I won't go with him! I won't!"

"Don't be so insolent," said Mr. Bumble.

"I've heard about chimney sweeps," Oliver said. "You can die up a chimney. They light a fire to make you hurry down, and you get smothered in the smoke."

"Nonsense!" said Mr. Gamfield. "I just gets a nice crackling blaze going and the boys come down quicker than anything."

15

Pause after page 15.

Note the word "laden", and check the children's understanding.

- Why does the sweep need a small boy?
- Note "smothered in smoke", and later "frizzle in flames" (page 16). Can the children spot and label the alliteration?

Now ask the children to read on to page 16.

"Then I'll frizzle in flames. I'm not going," replied Oliver firmly.

Mr. Gamfield clambered back into his donkey cart. "I don't want a rebellious boy. You've spoiled him, Mr. Bumble."

With that, he whipped the donkey until it trotted away.

Mr. Bumble shook Oliver until his teeth rattled. "Keep your mouth shut or no one will want you," he bellowed. "You've ruined that chance. Don't ruin the next. Look! Here it comes now."

He pointed to a thin, spidery man coming up to the door.

The man had a gloomy air. "I am Mr. Sowerberry," he introduced himself. "I arrange funerals and I need help." He looked at Oliver closely. "This boy will do, but he's so thin, he's not worth five pounds. I'll give you three pounds for him. Take it or leave it."

16

Pause after page 16.

Tell the children Dickens loved to make up interesting names for his characters.

- Do you think '"Mr. Sowerberry" is a good name? Why?
  (Think about the associations: "sour" and "bury".)

Now ask the children to read on to page 20.

Mr. Bumble was disgusted, but there was nothing he could do. He was eager to see the last of Oliver. "Glad you're going, Oliver. Behave, or else..." he threatened.

Back at his shop, Mr. Sowerberry showed Oliver a dusty basement. A dim light filtered in, through a grimy pane of glass barred with rusty iron rails.

"You'll sleep here, you little bag of bones," he said.

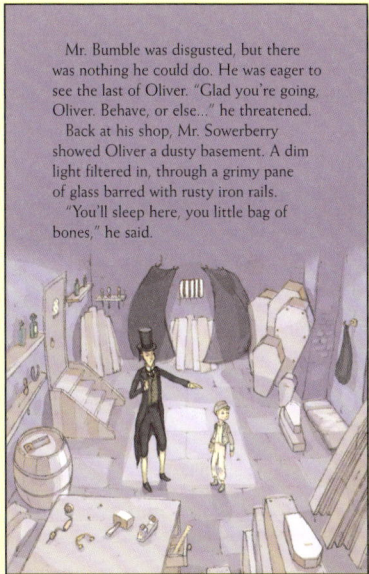

page 17

Oliver looked around the shadowy room. It was stacked with empty coffins and planks of wood. Drapes of black cloth hung from hooks in the walls, billowing occasionally in the breeze, as though first they breathed... and then were lifeless. The only place to sleep – a recess behind the coffins where a thin mattress was thrust – looked like a grave.

"And this is Noah, my apprentice," Mr. Sowerberry went on, taking him to the kitchen. "Noah, give Oliver his supper."

Noah looked cross. "What work is he going to do?" he asked, sulkily.

"He'll be a mute. He's a good-looking boy. Dressed in a top hat and mourning clothes, he'll be a credit to the business."

"Please sir, what's a mute?" asked Oliver.

"A mute walks next to the coffin at funerals and follows it to the grave. Children's funerals only. Winter's coming on – the sickly season. Always lots of children's funerals this time of year..."

Noah grinned unpleasantly when Mr. Sowerberry left them alone. "Here's your food." He handed Oliver the dog's bowl. Stuck to the side were some stinking scraps of cold fat the dog had rejected. Oliver was so hungry, he wolfed them down.

pages 18-19

"Pig!" mocked Noah. "Workhouse Boy! If your mother hadn't died, she'd be in prison. She must have been bad. Only bad 'uns give birth in the workhouse."

"Don't you dare say anything against my mother!" shouted Oliver.

"So? What are you going to do about it?" Noah jeered.

"This!" Oliver punched Noah hard in his flabby stomach. Noah collapsed like a crumpled balloon.

20

Pause after page 20.
You might say:

- Why do you think Noah, the apprentice, is so unkind to Oliver?

- Why does Oliver finally attack him?

"Ow!" he squealed. "HELP! MURDER! Mr. Sowerberry? You've lost your mind, Oliver Twist. You just wait, Workhouse Boy. You'll be punished for this."

"Do what you want," replied Oliver. "I'm not staying here any longer." He raced out of the door and tore down the road, his heart pounding. "Don't let them come after me," he prayed.

page 21

Pause after page 21.
Ask the children to report back on two facts they have learned from this chapter.

Suggested session 2

You might like to go over the story so far. What do the children remember from the previous session? Look through the first part of the book to refresh their memories.

When you are ready, ask the children to read chapters 4 and 5 (pages 22-44), whilst you monitor and record strategies.

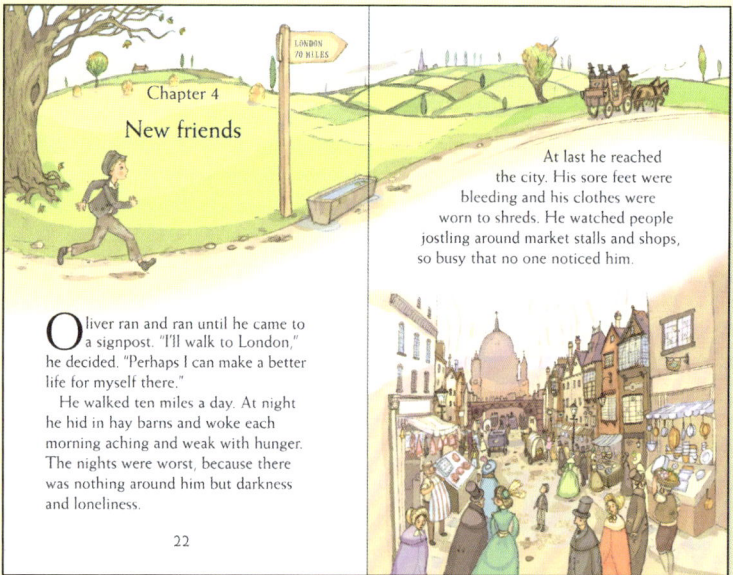

Chapter 4

New friends

Oliver ran and ran until he came to a signpost. "I'll walk to London," he decided. "Perhaps I can make a better life for myself there."

He walked ten miles a day. At night he hid in hay barns and woke each morning aching and weak with hunger. The nights were worst, because there was nothing around him but darkness and loneliness.

22

At last he reached the city. His sore feet were bleeding and his clothes were worn to shreds. He watched people jostling around market stalls and shops, so busy that no one noticed him.

Pause after page 23.

- Oliver's life so far has been in the workhouse and, for a short spell, with Mr. Sowerberry. What must it be like for him arriving in London for the first time?

On pages 23-26, there are lots of clues about what London was like in Victorian times.

- What can you find out from the text and the pictures?

Now ask the children to read on to page 31.

He collapsed on a cold doorstep, too exhausted to beg. Delicious smells floated by from a bakery. Oliver staggered up to the window, where shelves groaned with piles of freshly-made bread, cakes, buns and pies. He stared at them longingly.

A boy about the same age, with sharp eyes and a swaggering walk, strolled over. "Hungry?" he asked.

"Very," gasped Oliver.

To Oliver's astonishment, the boy pulled a wad of money out of his pocket. "I'll get you something. Wait here."

The boy returned with a bag crammed with hot meat pies.

"I'm Dodger," said the boy, as Oliver gobbled the food. "You?"

"Oliver Twist."

"Got a bed tonight, Oliver?"

"No."

pages 24-25

"Got any family?"

"No one at all."

"I know a kind gentleman who'll take you in. He won't want any rent, either."

"That's generous!" exclaimed Oliver. He followed Dodger down a maze of narrow alleys, where foul smells filled the air and swarms of ragged urchins played in slimy, oozing gutters. Men and women staggered around, cursing loudly.

It looked so dirty, Oliver almost wished he hadn't come, but he had nowhere else to go. Finally, they reached a crumbling house. Dodger led him up a rickety staircase to a dark room.

Through a cloud of sizzling fumes, Oliver spied a gnarled old man. He was wearing a grubby blue coat and frying sausages over the fire.

27

Behind him, a group of boys danced and dodged, playing a game. The old man's coat had lots of pockets, stuffed with hankies, wallets and pens and the boys were trying to pull them out without him noticing.

"Hey, Fagin," yelled Dodger. "This is Oliver."

"Hello, Oliver." Fagin bared his teeth in a leering grin. "Want to play?"

"Yes sir," said Oliver politely. He waited until Fagin bent over the frying pan, crept up... and delicately drew out a hanky.

"You're a natural!" chuckled Fagin. "Come near the fire. Have a sausage!"

Another man stepped in, smearing the back of his dirty hand across his mouth. With him were a girl and a snarling dog with a scratched, torn face.

"Ah, Bill Sikes," drawled Fagin. "Delighted to see you! What can I do for you and Nancy?"

"Give Bullseye supper," Bill growled, kicking his dog. "And get me a drink."

"Get to work, boys," Fagin ordered. One found a bone for the dog, while Dodger gave Nancy a half-full jug of gin. She emptied it into a brimming mug and passed it to Bill.

"Bill's scary," Oliver thought, snuggling under his blanket that night. "But I'm lucky to have found new friends."

29

24

"Good boy," said Fagin, letting go. "Keep quiet, or you'll be sorry. That's all I have to keep me in my old age. Do what you're told, Oliver, if you want to be happy here."

A few days later, Fagin told Oliver to go out with Dodger. They stopped by a bookshop which had a stall outside in the street. A richly-dressed gentleman had picked up a book from the stall and was reading it as hard as if he was in his study.

The next morning, waking in the pale half-light of dawn, Oliver saw Fagin open a chest and run his hands over necklaces, sparkling rings and shining gold coins.

Fagin turned to face Oliver's gaze. He thrust the chest back under the floor, seized a knife and pressed the blade into Oliver's neck.

"What did you see?" he hissed.

"Nothing," stammered Oliver, terrified.

pages 30-31

Pause after the first paragraph on page 31 ("...if you want to be happy here").

- On page 28, Fagin asks Oliver if he wants to play. Do you think it was really a game? What do you think the boys were doing?

- Where do you think Fagin's treasure comes from?

- What might happen next?

Now ask the children to read on to page 34.

"See him?" asked Dodger. "Prime target. Stick by me."

With one slick move, Dodger pulled a wallet from the gentleman's coat pocket.

In that moment, Oliver saw what his new friends were. Thieves!

Chapter 5

Betrayed

The gentleman spun around, realizing he'd been robbed. "STOP THIEF!" he yelled at Oliver.

Oliver looked for Dodger but he'd vanished. Panicking, Oliver raced off, followed by every man and woman in the street.

pages 32-33

"STOP THIEF!" they shouted, chasing him helter-skelter through mud and puddles, throwing sticks and stones at his scrawny back.

Oliver, breathless, kept running until a stone struck his head. He fell down, stunned. "Please sir," he whispered, as the gentleman reached him. "I'm not a thief."

Pause after page 34.

- Make sure the children understand "scrawny".

Now ask the children to read on to page 37.

page 34

The gentleman stared at him. "Hmm... Well, you look honest. Indeed, you look like–" He stopped, puzzled. "I'm sure I know that face," he murmured

"Get the police," said a passer-by.

"No. He deserves a chance," replied the gentleman. "Who are you, boy? My name's Brownlow. Perhaps I can help you. Come with me."

Mr. Brownlow took Oliver to his grand house. In the hallway was a portrait of a beautiful girl. Oliver stopped and stared at it, drinking it in.

"That was my niece, Agnes," said Mr. Brownlow. "She had a sad life. I wish she'd come to me for help. She must be dead now, poor girl." He looked at the portrait, then at Oliver. "I can't believe it," he muttered. "The likeness is extraordinary... Where were you born?" he asked urgently.

36

"In Mr. Bumble's workhouse," Oliver replied, surprised at the sudden question.

"Yes, I've heard of it," said Mr. Brownlow, nodding and looking grim. "Now, tell me about yourself."

Oliver recounted his life story, up until the moment he ran from the bookshop.

"I believe you," said Mr. Brownlow. He put his hands on Oliver's shoulders and looked down at him. "Would you like to live here and go to school?"

"Really?" gasped Oliver. "Truly?"

Mr. Brownlow laughed. "I'll have Mrs. Bedwin, my housekeeper, show you to your room."

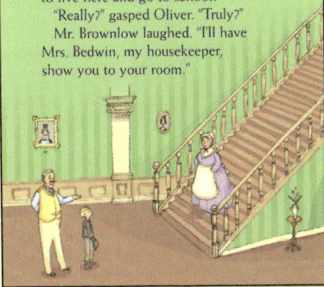

Pause after page 37.

Ask the children to speculate why Mr. Brownlow believes that Oliver is not a thief, and why he takes him in to live with him.

Now ask the children to read on to page 44.

"You poor child," sighed Mrs. Bedwin, as she took Oliver upstairs. "So dirty and ragged. Have a hot bath and I'll get you some clean clothes."

Lying in bed that night Oliver had never felt happier. And, as the weeks passed, he grew happier still. Mrs. Bedwin looked after him, from a good breakfast each morning to a hug last thing at night. Mr. Brownlow played games with him, shared his books and taught him chess and music.

"I feel as if I'm living in a dream," thought Oliver.

A few weeks later, Mr. Brownlow summoned him to his study. "Here's five pounds and some books. Will you take them to the bookshop where we met?"

"Of course," replied Oliver. "I'll do anything for you!"

"And come straight home," Mr. Brownlow said.

"I'll run there and back again," Oliver promised. He ran down the front steps and waved goodbye to Mrs. Bedwin, who was watching him from the window.

"Bless him," she thought. "I can't bear to let him out of my sight."

Oliver whistled as he strolled down the street. Suddenly, a pair of arms seized him tightly around the neck.

"OW!" he yelled. "Let go."

"Oh, Oliver, you naughty boy! I've found you."

Oliver was astonished. It was Nancy, Bill Sikes' friend. "Nancy – is that you? What are you doing here?"

41

A crowd gathered, staring at them.

"He's my little runaway brother," Nancy announced in a silky, false voice.

"But..." Oliver began.

Bill Sikes shot out of a beer shop with his snarling dog and grabbed Oliver.

"Watch him, Bullseye," he hissed. Bullseye seized Oliver's leg and hung on to it with his sharp teeth.

"I don't belong to these people!" shouted Oliver, struggling to get away. "I have to go back to Mr. Brownlow."

42

But Nancy quickly covered his mouth until he nearly suffocated.

Bill dragged him through the alleyways, Bullseye growling at Oliver's every step, until they reached Fagin's attic.

"Good of you to drop in, Oliver," drawled Fagin sarcastically.

"Fancy clothes," laughed Dodger.

"Expensive books! We'll sell everything," crowed Fagin. He examined Oliver's pockets. "Aha! Even better. Here's five pounds."

"Mine," growled Bill.

"No, mine, surely," contradicted Fagin, but Bill snatched it away.

"It's Mr. Brownlow's," said Oliver bitterly. "Let me go," he begged. "Or Mr. Brownlow will think I'm a thief."

Fagin patted his head. "We'll make you one soon."

"NO!" Oliver shouted. "Why do you want me anyway?"

"So you can't tell tales," sneered Bill. "Once you're one of us, you won't dare tell the police. Now shut up."

44

Pause after page 44.

You might ask:

- Why do Nancy and Bill kidnap Oliver?
- What can you tell about Bill and Fagin and what they think of children?

Suggested session 3

Go over the story so far. What do the children remember from the previous sessions? Look through the first part of the book to refresh their memories.

When you are ready, ask the children to read chapters 6 and 7 (pages 45-63), whilst you monitor and record strategies.

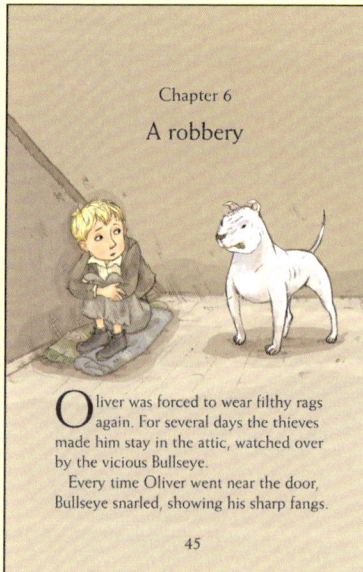

Chapter 6

A robbery

Oliver was forced to wear filthy rags again. For several days the thieves made him stay in the attic, watched over by the vicious Bullseye.
Every time Oliver went near the door, Bullseye snarled, showing his sharp fangs.

45

"Don't set the dog on him, Bill," Nancy begged. "You've got Oliver back. You don't have to frighten him now."

"Oh don't I?" snarled Bill. He brandished a pistol. "See this, Oliver?"

Oliver nodded nervously.

"It's loaded. If you don't do what you're told, I'll fire. Understand?"

"Yes, Bill," said Oliver, trembling.

page 46

Pause after page 46.
- Ask if the children already know what "brandished" means. If not, can they work it out (from the context, and the picture)?
- Can you think of other verbs (e.g. "held", "pointed") that could be used instead?
- Are they as powerful?

Now ask the children to read on to page 49.

"Good. There's a job I want to do tonight. Big house, loaded with silver and jewels. They keep a small window open and I need a scrap of a boy to slip through it and undo the door locks."

"He means what he says about the gun," advised Fagin. "Don't try and cross Bill Sikes."

When night fell, Bill dragged Oliver to the house. They hid under a bush until the church clock struck midnight. It was intensely dark.

47

Bill hoisted Oliver up to a tiny window. "Get in," he hissed.

"Please don't make me steal," implored Oliver.

Sikes raised his fist. "Do it, or I'll bash your head in."

He shoved Oliver through the window, lit a lantern and handed it to him. "Open the front door," he ordered. "There's a bolt at the top you won't reach, so stand on one of the chairs. Remember, you're in my gunshot range."

Oliver saw Bill's pistol aimed at him. He had no choice: he crept inside and went to unlock the door.

As he slid back the bolt, he heard Bill running around to the front of the house.

"I must warn the family, somehow," Oliver thought. "I don't care what happens to me." And he dropped the lantern with a clatter.

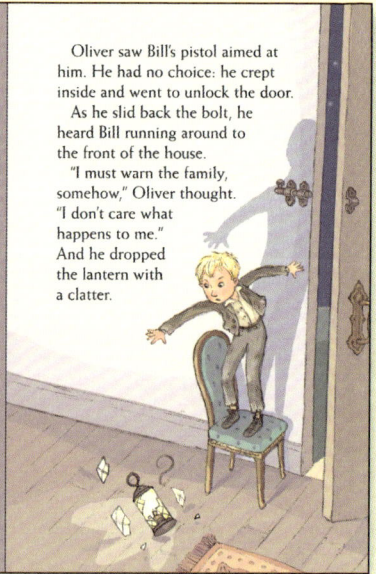

pages 48-49

Pause after pages 48-49.

Oliver is determined to alert the family to the break-in.

- Is dropping the lantern a brave or a foolish thing to do?

- What does this tell us about his character?

Now ask the children to read on to page 54.

After that, everything seemed to happen at once. Bill burst in to grab Oliver, a man appeared with a gun, and both men fired.

Oliver screamed, caught in the crossfire. He clutched his arm and saw his sleeve turn red.

Bill dragged him outside. "You fool," he growled. "They'll be after us. RUN!"

But Oliver, his arm throbbing, lagged behind. Bill flung him into a ditch. "You're too slow," he yelled down at him. "You can die here."

When Bill finally reached Fagin's house, Nancy rushed up to him. "How did it go?" she asked.

"Disaster," said Bill curtly. "Get me a drink."

"Where's the boy, Bill?"

"Dying in a ditch somewhere."

"You can't leave him there," Nancy cried. "I'll go and find him."

Bill lurched to his feet. "Don't you dare, Nancy!" But Nancy had already grabbed her cloak and was running through the door. A crafty look spread over Bill's face.

"After her, Bullseye," he ordered. "She won't get away with this."

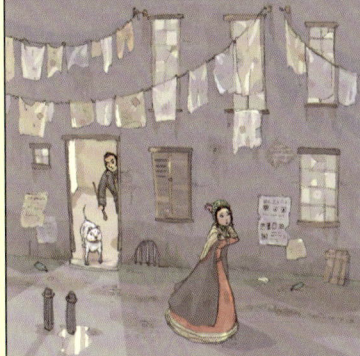

Nancy ran to the house Bill had tried to rob and searched everywhere for Oliver. At last she found him, weak and shivering.

"Thank you for coming," he muttered. She quickly bandaged his bleeding arm with her shawl. "I found your friend Mr. Brownlow. I'll take you to him," she whispered. "He'll be waiting for us on London Bridge."

"I don't believe you," Oliver said. "It's a trick."

"It isn't, Oliver, I promise. I met Mr. Brownlow yesterday. It's all arranged."

"Why are you doing this?"

"I've worked for Fagin since I was little. I don't want you to suffer like me."

"Stay with me," Oliver urged her. "Mr. Brownlow will look after you too. We could both start a new life."

"I can't leave Bill," Nancy shrugged. "I know he's bad, but I love him. Besides," she added, "I've been a thief all my life. It's too late to change now."

"It's never too late," said Oliver.

page 54

Pause after page 54.

You might say:

- We have seen a different side of Nancy's character in this chapter. Why do you think she goes to rescue Oliver but can't leave Bill and Fagin?

Now ask the children to read page 55.

They hurried through the dark streets where flickering gas lamps shone eerie shafts of light on the cobbles.

Neither of them saw the dog following them – a dog with a scratched torn face and an eager snarling mouth. And behind the dog, a man, who moved with silent, stealthy footsteps through the shadows.

page 55

Pause again after page 55.

- Ask the children to look carefully at the way suspense is built up on this page.
- Can they pick out particularly effective words and phrases (e.g. "flickering gas lamps", "eerie shafts of light", "silent, stealthy footsteps")?

Now ask the children to read on to page 63.

Chapter 7

The secret of the locket

They reached the bridge at dawn. Mr. Brownlow was waiting, just as Nancy had promised. "Run!" she cried to Oliver.

Oliver dashed forward. He'd almost reached Mr. Brownlow's outstretched arms when Nancy's frightened voice made him turn around.

"W-why did you follow me, Bill?" Nancy stuttered. "I told no tales – I'd never grass on you."

"You took the boy away," Bill bellowed. "You betrayed me, Nancy. I can't ever trust you again."

Then Oliver heard Nancy scream. "No! Please, Bill, NO!"

BANG! A pistol shot exploded and Nancy slumped lifeless to the ground. Bill swore and closed his eyes. "I had to kill her," he muttered.

Oliver was frozen to the spot with terror.

"I'm here, Oliver," said Mr. Brownlow, reassuringly. "Come to me. Don't look."

By now, a crowd had appeared, drawn by the sound of the pistol shot. Bill fled from the bridge, desperate to escape.

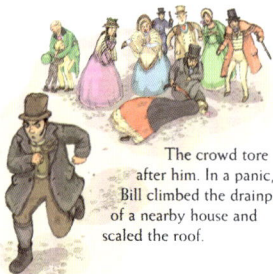

The crowd tore after him. In a panic, Bill climbed the drainpipe of a nearby house and scaled the roof.

He grabbed a rope that was dangling from its chimney, intending to swing over to the roof of the house opposite. Quickly, he made a loop and slipped it over his head. But before he could bring it down his body and under his arms, a policeman sounded his whistle below.

"Stop him!" cried a woman. "He's getting away."

Bill lost his balance and tumbled off the roof, the rope tightening around his neck. In seconds, he was dead, his body swaying in mid-air.

Bullseye ran back and forth, howling dismally. Then the dog leaped at the dead man, trying to reach him. Instead, he dashed his head on a stone windowsill and fell to the ground. The dog was as dead as his master.

Mr. Brownlow held Oliver firmly in his arms. Oliver couldn't stop shaking.

"Nothing can hurt you now," Mr. Brownlow told him. "You're safe. Bill deserved that, for what he did to Nancy."

"Poor Nancy," Oliver sobbed.

"Yes, she was a brave girl." He hugged Oliver tightly. "Listen, Oliver, I have good news for both of us. I went to see Mr. Bumble and he gave me this." He handed Oliver a gold locket. "Open it."

Oliver looked at the inscription inside. "Agnes," he read.

"Mrs. Mann, the midwife who was with your mother at the workhouse, stole this locket from her. Later, Mrs. Mann married Mr. Bumble. That's how he discovered the locket."

pages 60-61

36

"Was Agnes my mother?" Oliver asked.
"Yes. Your mother and my niece. I gave her the locket many years ago – I recognized it at once. You remember her portrait at home? You look just like her."
Mr. Brownlow hugged Oliver again. "You're my boy now," he said.
"Do I really belong to you?" Oliver asked, hardly daring to believe it.

Mr. Brownlow smiled. "You really do. Please God, your unhappy life is over forever. Let's go, Oliver. Mrs. Bedwin is longing to see you again."
And, hand-in-hand, they walked home.

pages 62-63

Pause after page 63.

You might say:

- The story ends happily for Oliver. But what about the Artful Dodger and Fagin? What might happen to them?

  (Encourage the children to draw on what they have learnt about life in London for children at this time, as well as Bill Sikes' fate.)

Now return to the text (see over the page) to discuss whether the children's answers and predictions were correct, and talk about their approaches.

37

Return to the text

The return to the text allows you to reinforce teaching points, e.g. checking children's understanding, identifying and reinforcing successful decoding strategies.

Look through the story again to recap on strategies the children have used for decoding unfamiliar words (e.g. phonic, graphic, context or syntax).
You might say:

· I really liked the way (*child's name*) worked out how to read (*word or phrase*) – can you tell us how you did it?

Talk about the story as a whole. You might ask:

· Were there any parts of the story that surprised you?

· Which part (or character or picture) did you like best?

· Did you like the ending? Can you think of a different way the story could have ended?

· Do you know any other stories like this?
You needn't only consider other Dickens novels or Dickensian backgrounds: think about similar characters and settings, as well as plot and period.

Further reading

Oliver Twist is in **Series Three** of the **Usborne Young Reading** series. These are some of the other titles in Series Three, including **Great Expectations**, another of Dickens' best-loved novels.

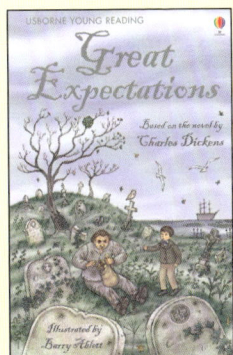

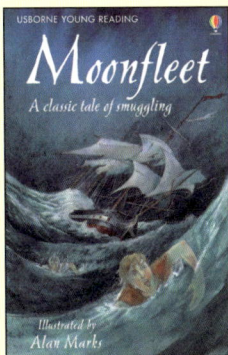

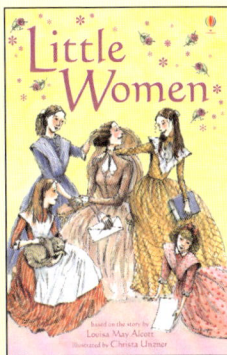

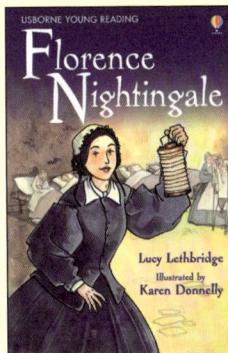

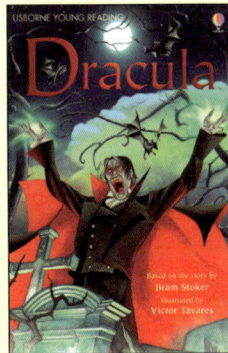

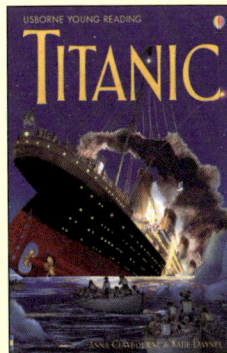

There are over 100 titles available in the Young Reading series, and more are being added all the time. To find out about all the titles available, go to **www.usborne.com**

Guided Reading Record

Text: *Oliver Twist – National Curriculum Level 4A*

Class: ....

Group: ....

Date: ....

Teacher/
Teaching Assistant: ....

At Level 4A, it is expected that children:

1. Read for different purposes using appropriate strategies.

2. Distinguish between fact and fiction.

3. Confidently read with a range of expression relevant to the genre, purpose and audience.

4. Respond to a range of texts with understanding of significant ideas, themes and events, based on inference and deduction.

5. Refer to text when giving views.

6. Locate and use ideas from a wide range of sources of information.

Name: *Comments:* *Target:*	*Name:* *Comments:* *Target:*
Name: *Comments:* *Target:*	*Name:* *Comments:* *Target:*
Name: *Comments:* *Target:*	*Name:* *Comments:* *Target:*

About the Usborne Reading Programme

The Usborne Reading Programme is a collection of over 150 titles for beginner readers, graded in seven levels from very beginners to fully confident readers. Launched in 2002, it has since sold almost 5 million copies worldwide.

The Usborne Reading Programme combines vivid, engaging writing with captivating full-colour illustration on every page. From classic tales to lively non-fiction, there is something to appeal to everyone.

From one level to the next, there is a clear progression in terms of subject, style, narrative length, sentence structure and vocabulary, giving children the satisfaction of mastering real books and making measurable progress without overstretching them and causing them to lose enthusiasm.

Non-fiction titles at all levels draw on the expertise of a range of specialists in their subject, ensuring that the books are not only engaging but authoritative: for example, Eva Schloss, stepsister of Anne Frank, advised on **Anne Frank**, and John Woolley of the Captain Cook Memorial Museum in Whitby advised on **Captain Cook**.

The Reading Programme advisers

The Reading Programme has been developed in consultation with **Alison Kelly**, a leading expert in the teaching of reading, who helped to draw up the seven-level framework (see pages 46-47). Alison worked for many years as a primary school teacher in London, and is currently a Senior Lecturer in Education at Roehampton University, teaching about all aspects of literacy.

Suzanne Maile is assistant headteacher at Sheen Mount Primary School in south-west London, a thriving school with a reputation for outstanding teaching and learning. Suzanne is responsible for curriculum development and initial teacher training at Sheen Mount, and has extensive experience in teaching guided reading at all levels. She is also a teacher tutor at Roehampton University, and a consultant teacher for Richmond LEA.

Together, Suzanne and Alison have chosen a selection of titles from the Reading Programme that are particularly suitable for guided reading, and produced comprehensive teacher's notes, packed with ideas and guidance for guided reading sessions.

The range of titles in the Reading Programme provides wide scope for further reading at every level.

The Usborne Reading Programme and the National Curriculum

The Usborne Reading Progamme is fully integrated with the National Curriculum for English at Key Stages 1 and 2, encouraging children to develop fluent and accurate reading across a range of texts, subjects and styles.

Selected titles from all levels of the Reading Programme are available as Guided Reading packs, comprising six copies of the book plus comprehensive teacher's notes. Guided Reading packs represent a selection of text types, and are carefully graded within levels 1-4 of the National Curriculum.

Text type:
European folktale
NC level: 1C

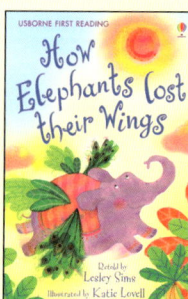

Text type:
Asian folktale
NC level: 1B

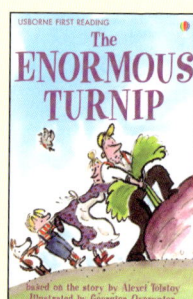

Text type: adapted
children's classic
NC level: 1A

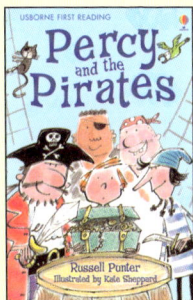

Text type:
original fiction
NC level: 2C

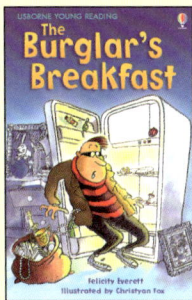

Text type:
original fiction
NC level: 2B

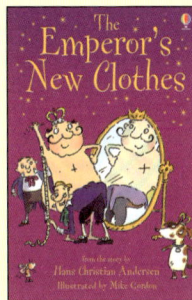

Text type:
classic fairytale
NC level: 2A

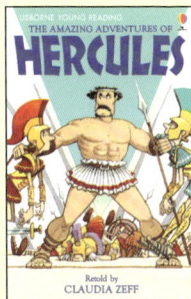

Text type:
myths and legends
NC level: 3C

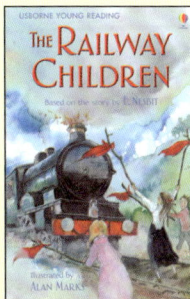

Text type: adapted
children's classic
NC level: 3B

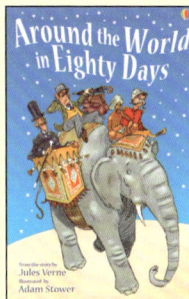

Text type:
adapted classic
NC level: 3A

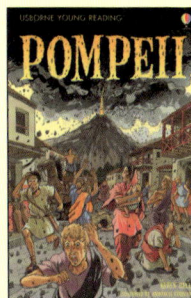

Text type:
non-fiction (history)
NC level: 4C

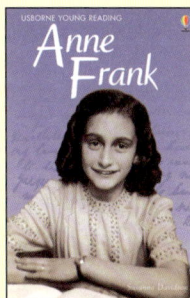

Text type:
biography
NC level: 4B

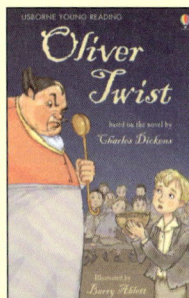

Text type:
adapted classic
NC level: 4A

The Usborne Reading

	Number of words	Themes
First Reading Level One National Curriculum level 1	up to 150	Classic tales (e.g. Aesop's Fables) and folktales
First Reading Level Two National Curriculum level 1	up to 250	As Level One, including less familiar folktales
First Reading Level Three National Curriculum level 1-2	up to 450	As Level Two plus original fiction and non-fiction (natural history life cycles)
First Reading Level Four National Curriculum level 2	up to 750	As Level Three plus classic fairy tales
Young Reading Series One National Curriculum level 2-3	1,000-1,500	Fairy tales, fantasy, fiction, non-fiction ("the story of...")
Young Reading Series Two National Curriculum level 3	2,000-2,500	As Series One plus adapted classics
Young Reading Series Three National Curriculum level 3-4	3,000-5,000	History, biographies, classics

The elements above are intended as guidelines only, and whilst distinctions between different levels remain clear

Programme framework

Content	Vocabulary
Short single narrative followed by reading and comprehension puzzles	Simple everyday vocabulary, familiar items
Single narrative plus character sheets and/or maps, and puzzles	More descriptive and evocative vocabulary, always clear in context
Single narrative with repeated elements, plus character sheets and/or maps, no puzzles	Powerful verbs and adjectives, clear in context
Single narrative	More exotic elements and controlled use of idiom
Several linked stories or one longer narrative in chapters. Direct and indirect speech, intertextual references	Wide-ranging everyday vocabulary
Single narrative in chapters. Introduce irony and subplot, allow opportunity for inference and deduction	More challenging, building on Series One; specialist or technical terms explained
Single narrative in chapters. Assumes some relevant background knowledge	Building on Series Two, may assume knowledge of specialist or technical terms

exceptions may sometimes be made to individual specifications in the interests of narrative or style.

Edited by Mairi Mackinnon

Designed by Katarina Dragoslavic

First published in 2008 by Usborne Publishing Ltd.,
83-85 Saffron Hill, London ECIN 8RT, England. www.usborne.com
Copyright © 2008 Usborne Publishing Ltd.